MANIFEST
ABUNDANCE
WITH 369 METHOD

A 180-DAY MANIFESTING JOURNAL
AND GUIDED WORKBOOK

369 Project Manifestation With Guided
Questions, Positive Affirmation, And
The Power of The Law Of Attraction

Jaime Wishstone

Manifest Abundance With 369 Method by Jaime Wishstone

Published by Wishstone Trading Limited

Https://soldouthouses.com

Copyright © 2022 Jaime Wishstone

BONUS RESOURCES

Thanks for getting this book; here are some bonus resources that help you attract more wealth, love, and abundance to your life:

#1 Download your free report to discover 7 ancient secrets to manifest more wealth, love, and abundance into your life

Download your report at

https://manifestabundance.net/dreamlife

#2 Sign up for a free video training to discover how to manifest more wealth, love, and abundance into your life with the "untold method"

Sign up for the free training at

https://manifestabundance.net/freetraining

TABLE OF CONTENT

INTRODUCTION

Welcome to the **Manifest Abundance With 369 Method: A 180-Day Manifesting Journal And Guided Workbook**! This journal is designed to help you manifest your desires using the powerful 369 method and other manifestation techniques and practices.

The 369 method is a simple but effective approach to manifestation that involves repeating a specific affirmation or intention for a set amount of time each day. **By focusing your energy and attention on your desires in this way, you can start to shift your thoughts, beliefs, and actions toward creating the reality you want.**

This journal and workbook is divided into several sections that will guide you through the process of using the 369 method and other manifestation practices to achieve your goals.

In section 1, you'll learn more about the history and benefits of the 369 method, and how it works. In section 2, you'll prepare to manifest by clarifying your desires, setting achievable goals, and creating affirmations to support your manifestations.

In section 3, you'll use the 369 method to focus your energy and attention on your desires with step-by-step guidance and examples. In section 4, you'll enhance your manifestation practice by exploring additional tools and techniques, such as meditation, visualization, and gratitude practices. In section 5, you'll troubleshoot any challenges or obstacles to your manifestation practice with strategies and tips to help you stay motivated and consistent.

This journal and workbook is designed to be a supportive and empowering tool for your manifestation journey. By using it regularly and consistently, you'll start to see positive changes in your thoughts, beliefs, and actions, leading to the manifestation of your desires. Remember to be patient, kind, and compassionate with yourself throughout the process, and celebrate your progress and successes along the way.

Let's begin!

SECTION 1

UNDERSTANDING THE 369 METHOD

INTRODUCTION TO THE 369 METHOD

The 369 method is a powerful manifestation technique that has gained popularity in recent years. It's a simple yet effective approach to manifesting your desires by focusing your energy and attention on a specific affirmation or intention for a set amount of time each day. In this chapter, we'll explore the history and benefits of the 369 method, and how it works.

History and Origin of the 369 Method

The 369 method is based on the teachings of Nikola Tesla, a famous inventor and physicist who lived in the late 19th and early 20th centuries. Tesla is known for his contributions to the development of modern technology, including the invention of alternating current (AC) electricity. But he was also a philosopher and mystic who believed in the power of the human mind to create reality.

According to some sources, Tesla developed the 369 method as a way to tap into the creative potential of the universe and manifest his desires. The method is based on the idea that all things in the universe vibrate at different frequencies, and that by aligning your thoughts and emotions with the frequency of your desires, you can attract them into your life.

How the 369 Method Works

The 369 method is a simple three-step process that involves repeating a specific affirmation or intention for a set amount of time each day. Here's how it works:

Step 1: Choose your affirmation or intention. This should be a clear and specific statement that reflects your desired outcome. For example, "I am abundant and prosperous," or "I attract loving and supportive relationships."

Step 2: Repeat the affirmation or intention three times in the morning, six times in the afternoon, and nine times in the evening. This can be done silently or out loud, and should be accompanied by a feeling of gratitude and positive emotion.

Step 3: Continue this practice for 21 days or longer, until your desired outcome is manifested.

The idea behind the 369 method is that by repeating your affirmation or intention in this way, you're sending a clear and consistent message to the universe about what you want to attract into your life. The repetition also helps to reinforce positive beliefs and emotions, and to replace any negative thoughts or limiting beliefs that may be holding you back from success.

Benefits of the 369 Method

There are many benefits to using the 369 method for manifestation. Here are just a few:

- It's a simple and easy-to-use technique that can be done anywhere, anytime.
- It helps to focus your energy and attention on your desired outcome, making it easier to achieve.
- It reinforces positive beliefs and emotions, which can have a ripple effect on other areas of your life.
- It can help to shift your mindset from one of limitation to one of abundance and possibility.
- It's a powerful tool for personal growth and self-discovery.

The 369 method is a simple but powerful tool for manifestation that can help you to attract your desires and create the reality you want. In the next chapter, we'll explore the importance of setting clear intentions and identifying your true desires, as well as tips for using the 369 method in your daily life.

THE POWER OF INTENTION

Why Setting Clear Intentions is Important

Setting clear intentions is an essential part of any manifestation practice, including the 369 method. When you have a clear and specific goal in mind, you're more likely to take action and make decisions that are aligned with that goal. You're also sending a clear and consistent message to the universe about what you want to attract into your life.

On the other hand, if you're unclear or vague about your intentions, you may end up attracting mixed or contradictory results. For example, if you say you want to attract more money, but you're not clear about how much money you want or what you'll do with it, you may end up manifesting unexpected or undesired outcomes.

Tips for Setting Clear Intentions

Here are some tips to help you set clear intentions for your manifestation practice:

1. **Be specific:** Choose a specific outcome that you want to manifest, and be as clear and detailed as possible about what it looks like.
2. **Focus on what you wan**t, not what you don't want: Instead of focusing on what you don't want, focus on what you do want. For example, instead of saying "I don't want to be in debt," say "I am financially free and abundant."
3. **Use positive language**: Use positive language in your affirmations and intentions, as if you've already achieved your desired outcome. For example, say "I am" or "I have," rather than "I will" or "I want."
4. **Align your intentions** with your values: Make sure your intentions are aligned with your core values and beliefs. If your intentions conflict with your values, you may have a hard time manifesting them.

Identifying Your True Desires

In addition to setting clear intentions, it's important to identify your true desires and goals. This means being clear about what you really want, rather than what you think you should want or what others expect of you.

Here are some prompts to help you identify your true desires:

1. What makes you happy? Think about the activities, people, and situations that bring you joy and fulfillment.
2. What are you passionate about? What gets you excited and energized?
3. What are your values and beliefs? What's important to you, and what do you stand for?
4. What do you want to contribute to the world? What impact do you want to make?

By being clear about your true desires, you can set powerful and authentic intentions that are aligned with your highest good.

THE SCIENCE OF MANIFESTATION

Manifestation is often seen as a mystical or magical process, but there is actually a science behind it. The following are some of the key principles of manifestation and how they relate to the 369 method.

The Law of Attraction

One of the most well-known principles of manifestation is the Law of Attraction. This law states that like attracts like, meaning that the energy you put out into the universe will be reflected back to you. In other words, if you focus on positive thoughts and feelings, you'll attract positive outcomes, and vice versa.

The Law of Vibration

The Law of Vibration is closely related to the Law of Attraction. This law states that everything in the universe is made up of energy and vibrates at a certain frequency. Your thoughts, emotions, and beliefs also have their own unique vibration. By aligning your thoughts and emotions with your desired outcome, you can raise your vibration and attract what you want into your life.

The Power of Visualization

Visualization is a powerful tool for manifestation. When you visualize your desired outcome, you're sending a clear and consistent message to the universe about what you want. This helps to align your thoughts and emotions with your desired outcome, making it more likely to manifest for you.

The Role of Belief

Belief is a crucial component of manifestation. If you don't believe that you can achieve your desired outcome, it's unlikely that you will. On the other hand, if you have a strong belief in yourself and your ability to manifest what you want, you're much more likely to succeed.

How the 369 Method Incorporates These Principles

The 369 method incorporates many of these principles of manifestation. By setting clear intentions and focusing on your desired outcome, you're aligning your thoughts and emotions with what you want to manifest. By repeating your affirmations in the morning, afternoon, and evening, you're sending a consistent message to the universe about what you want. And by incorporating gratitude into your practice, you're raising your vibration and attracting more abundance into your life.

Conclusion

In this chapter, we explored some of the key principles of manifestation and how they relate to the 369 method. By understanding the science behind manifestation, you can enhance your practice and increase your chances of success. In the next section, we'll dive deeper into the specifics of the 369 method and how to use it effectively for manifestation.

HOW TO USE THE 369 METHOD FOR MANIFESTATION

Now that we've explored the principles of manifestation and how they relate to the 369 method, let's dive deeper into how to use this method effectively for manifesting your desires. In this chapter, we'll go through the step-by-step process of using the 369 method.

Step 1: Setting Your Intention

The first step of the 369 method is to set your intention. Take some time to think about what you want to manifest, and be as specific as possible. Write your intention in the present tense as if it has already happened. For example, "I am grateful for the new job that pays me $X per year and allows me to work from home."

Step 2: Creating Your Affirmations

Next, you'll create three affirmations based on your intention. The first affirmation should be focused on what you want to achieve, the second on how you want to feel, and the third on what you're willing to give in return. For example:

1. "I am now attracting my dream job that pays me $X per year."
2. "I feel confident and fulfilled in my work every day."
3. "I am willing to put in the time and effort to excel in my new role."

Step 3: Repetition and Visualization

Once you've created your affirmations, you'll repeat them in the morning, afternoon, and evening. As you say each affirmation, visualize yourself already having achieved your desired outcome. See yourself in your new job, feeling happy and fulfilled, and putting in the effort to excel.

Step 4: Gratitude

Finally, end each repetition of your affirmations with a moment of gratitude. Express gratitude for the universe bringing you your desired outcome and the opportunities and resources that will help you achieve your goal.

TIPS AND GUIDANCE FOR EFFECTIVE USE OF THE 369 METHOD

While the 369 method can be a powerful tool for manifestation, it's important to use it effectively in order to see results. In this chapter, we'll provide some additional tips and guidance for getting the most out of the 369 method.

Tip 1: Stay Focused

One of the most important aspects of effective manifestation is staying focused on your desired outcome. Avoid getting distracted by negative thoughts or feelings, and stay committed to your affirmations and visualizations. If you find your mind wandering, take a few deep breaths and refocus on your intentions.

Tip 2: Be Consistent

Consistency is key when it comes to manifestation. Make sure to repeat your affirmations three times a day, every day, and visualize your desired outcome as often as possible. The more consistent you are with your practice, the more powerful it will become.

Tip 3: Use Positive Language

When creating your affirmations, it's important to use positive language. Focus on what you want to achieve, rather than what you want to avoid. For example, instead of saying "I don't want to be broke," say "I am attracting abundance and financial prosperity."

Tip 4: Stay Open to Opportunities

Manifestation is not about controlling every aspect of your life, but rather about opening yourself up to opportunities and possibilities. Stay open to unexpected opportunities and be willing to take action when they arise. Trust that the universe is working in your favor and that everything will unfold as it should.

Tip 5: Practice Gratitude

Gratitude is a key component of manifestation. By expressing gratitude for what you already have and what you are manifesting, you are raising your vibration and attracting more abundance into your life. Make gratitude a daily practice by keeping a gratitude journal or simply taking a few moments each day to express gratitude for the good things in your life.

In this chapter, we provided some additional tips and guidance for using the 369 method effectively. By staying focused, being consistent, using positive language, staying open to opportunities, and practicing gratitude, you can enhance your practice and increase your chances of success. In the next section, we'll provide some additional resources and exercises for further exploration and growth.

SECTION 2

PREPARING TO MANIFEST

STEP 1- CLARIFYING YOUR DESIRES AND INTENTIONS

Before you can effectively use the 369 methods to manifest your desires, it's important to take the time to clarify exactly what it is that you want. This chapter will guide you through the process of identifying your true desires and understanding the motivations behind them.

Identifying What You Truly Want

What makes you truly happy and fulfilled?

_____

_____

_____

_____

_____

_____

_____

_____

_____

_____

What activities do you enjoy doing that make you lose track of time?

_____

_____

_____

_____

_____

_____

_____

_____

_____

_____

If you could have anything you wanted in life, what would it be?

_____
_____
_____
_____
_____
_____
_____
_____
_____
_____

What are your biggest dreams and aspirations?

_____
_____
_____
_____
_____
_____
_____
_____
_____
_____

If you had unlimited resources and time, how would you spend your days?

_____

_____

_____

_____

_____

_____

_____

_____

_____

_____

What are the things that you've always wanted to do but never had the courage to pursue?

_____

_____

_____

_____

_____

_____

_____

_____

_____

_____

What are the things that you're passionate about?

_____

_____

_____

_____

_____

_____

_____

_____

_____

_____

What are the things that you value the most in life?

_____

_____

_____

_____

_____

_____

_____

_____

_____

_____

What are the things that you want to accomplish in the short-term and long term?

_____

_____

_____

_____

_____

_____

_____

_____

_____

_____

If you were to die tomorrow, what would you regret not having done or achieved?

_____

_____

_____

_____

_____

_____

_____

_____

_____

_____

Understanding the Motivation Behind Your Desires

Why do you want to manifest this desire?

_____

_____

_____

_____

_____

_____

_____

_____

_____

_____

What is the underlying reason behind your desire?

_____

_____

_____

_____

_____

_____

_____

_____

_____

_____

How will manifesting this desire improve your life?

What emotions do you hope to experience by manifesting this desire?

What is driving you to pursue this desire?

_____

_____

_____

_____

_____

_____

_____

_____

_____

_____

How will manifesting this desire align with your values and beliefs?

_____

_____

_____

_____

_____

_____

_____

_____

_____

_____

_____

What positive impact will manifesting this desire have on the people around you?

_____

_____

_____

_____

_____

_____

_____

_____

_____

_____

How will manifesting this desire help you grow and develop as a person?

_____

_____

_____

_____

_____

_____

_____

_____

_____

What challenges do you expect to face while manifesting this desire, and how will you overcome them?

_____

_____

_____

_____

_____

_____

_____

_____

_____

_____

Are there any potential negative consequences of manifesting this desire, and how will you address them?

_____

_____

_____

_____

_____

_____

_____

_____

_____

_____

Using Visualization to Clarify Your Intentions

What does your desired outcome look like?

_____

_____

_____

_____

_____

_____

_____

_____

_____

_____

How does it feel to have your desire manifested?

_____

_____

_____

_____

_____

_____

_____

_____

_____

_____

What emotions are associated with achieving your desired outcome?

_____

_____

_____

_____

_____

_____

_____

_____

_____

_____

What does your ideal day look like after manifesting your desire?

_____

_____

_____

_____

_____

_____

_____

_____

_____

_____

Who is present in your visualization? Are there any specific people or situations that are relevant to your manifestation?

What are you doing in your visualization? Can you see yourself taking specific actions towards your goal?

How does the environment around you look and feel in your visualization?

_____

_____

_____

_____

_____

_____

_____

_____

_____

_____

What are some obstacles that you may face while manifesting your desire, and how can you visualize overcoming them?

_____

_____

_____

_____

_____

_____

_____

_____

_____

_____

How can you incorporate your visualization practice into your daily routine to reinforce your intentions and beliefs?

By taking the time to clarify your desires and intentions, you'll be better equipped to use the 369 method to manifest your desired outcomes. This chapter will help you gain clarity and focus on what you truly want and why, setting the foundation for successful manifestation.

STEP 2- SETTING ACHIEVABLE GOALS

Once you've identified your desires and intentions, the next step is to set achievable goals that will help you manifest your desired outcomes. This chapter will guide you through the process of setting goals that are specific, measurable, achievable, relevant, and time-bound (SMART) to increase your chances of success.

Setting SMART Goals

Setting goals is a critical step in the manifestation process. By identifying what you want to achieve, you can create a roadmap for success and increase your focus and motivation. However, it's important to set goals that are specific, measurable, achievable, relevant, and time-bound, or SMART. This acronym provides a framework for creating goals that are effective and achievable.

The Five Components of SMART Goals

1. **Specific:** A specific goal is clear and well-defined. It answers the questions "what," "why," and "how."
2. **Measurable:** A measurable goal has a quantifiable outcome, which can be tracked and evaluated.
3. **Achievable:** An achievable goal is realistic and attainable. It requires effort and commitment but is not overly ambitious.
4. **Relevant:** A relevant goal is aligned with your values, interests, and aspirations. It is meaningful and significant to you.
5. **Time-bound:** A time-bound goal has a specific deadline or timeline for completion. It creates urgency and helps you stay focused.

Here are some examples of SMART goals for different areas of life:

- Career: "I will complete a professional certification in my field within the next six months to increase my marketability and earning potential."
- Health: "I will run a 5K race in three months by following a training plan and eating a healthy diet."
- Finances: "I will save $5,000 for a down payment on a house within the next year by creating a budget and reducing unnecessary expenses."
- Relationships: "I will improve communication with my partner by attending couples therapy twice a month for the next six months."
- Personal growth: "I will read one book per month for the next year to expand my knowledge and perspective."

How to Assess Whether a Goal is Truly Achievable

It's important to set goals that are challenging but still achievable. Here are some questions to help you assess whether a goal is truly achievable:

- Do you have the skills, knowledge, and resources needed to achieve this goal?
- Are there any obstacles or challenges that may prevent you from achieving this goal?
- Have you broken down the goal into smaller, manageable steps?
- Is the timeline for completing the goal realistic and achievable?

- Have you identified any potential risks or setbacks and created a plan to overcome them?

By using the SMART framework and assessing the achievability of your goals, you can set yourself up for success in your manifestation practice. Remember, setting goals is just one piece of the puzzle – you also need to take consistent action and believe in your ability to manifest your desires.

Setting

Specific: What exactly do you want to accomplish? Who is involved? What resources or limitations do you need to consider?

_____

_____

_____

_____

_____

_____

_____

_____

_____

Measurable: How will you measure progress towards your goal? What metrics will you use to determine success?

_____

_____

_____

_____

_____

_____

_____

_____

_____

Achievable: Is the goal realistically attainable given your current resources and limitations? What steps can you take to increase your chances of success?

_____

_____

_____

_____

_____

_____

_____

_____

_____

Relevant: Why is this goal important to you? How does it align with your values and overall vision for your life?

_____

_____

_____

_____

_____

_____

_____

_____

_____

Time-bound: What is your deadline for achieving this goal? Are there any milestones or checkpoints along the way?

Breaking Down Big Goals into Smaller, Achievable Steps

When we set big goals for ourselves, it can be overwhelming to know where to start. Breaking down these big goals into smaller, achievable steps is a powerful way to create momentum and build confidence as we work towards our desired outcome. Here are some strategies for breaking down big goals:

1. **Start with the end in mind:** Before breaking down your goal, it's important to clearly understand what your end result will look like. This will help you to identify the key steps you need to take to achieve your goal.

2. **Create a roadmap:** Once you clearly understand the end result, create a roadmap or plan for achieving your goal. This plan should include all the key steps that you need to take, along with timelines and deadlines.

3. **Prioritize the steps:** Not all steps are created equal. Some will be more important than others. Prioritize the steps in your plan based on what will have the biggest impact on achieving your goal.

4. **Break down each step:** Break it down further into smaller, achievable steps for each step in your plan. This will make it easier to focus on one task at a time and create a sense of progress.

5. **Celebrate progress:** Celebrate each small win along the way. This will help to keep you motivated and focused on achieving your goal.

Guided Questions:

What big goal do you want to achieve in your life?

_____

_____

_____

_____

_____

_____

_____

_____

_____

_____

What is the end result you want to achieve? Can you describe it in detail?

_____

_____

_____

_____

_____

_____

_____

_____

_____

_____

What are the key steps you need to take to achieve your goal?

_____

_____

_____

_____

_____

_____

_____

_____

_____

_____

How can you prioritize these steps based on their importance?

_____

_____

_____

_____

_____

_____

_____

_____

_____

_____

Can you break down each step into smaller, achievable steps?

_____

_____

_____

_____

_____

_____

_____

_____

_____

_____

How can you celebrate progress along the way?

_____

_____

_____

_____

_____

_____

_____

_____

_____

_____

Creating a Plan of Action to Achieve Your Goals

Once you have broken down your big goals into smaller, achievable steps, it's important to create a detailed plan of action to help you stay on track and focused. Here are some steps to help you create an effective plan:

1. **Set deadlines:** Determine when you want to achieve your goals and set deadlines for each step of your plan.
2. **Create a timeline:** Map out the specific actions you need to take and when you need to take them to reach your goals.
3. **Prioritize your tasks:** Focus on the most important tasks that will bring you closer to your goals and schedule them accordingly.
4. **Track your progress:** Regularly assess your progress towards your goals and adjust your plan if necessary.
5. **Stay motivated:** Keep yourself motivated by reminding yourself of your why and focusing on the positive changes that will come from achieving your goals.

Guided Questions:

What specific steps do I need to take to achieve my goal?

_____

_____

_____

_____

_____

_____

_____

_____

_____

_____

How can I break down my goal into smaller, achievable steps?

_____

_____

_____

_____

_____

_____

_____

_____

_____

What resources or support do I need to accomplish my goal?

How will I track my progress and hold myself accountable?

What potential obstacles or setbacks could I encounter, and how can I plan to overcome them?

_____

_____

_____

_____

_____

_____

_____

_____

_____

_____

How can I adjust my plan if necessary to ensure I stay on track towards achieving my goal?

_____

_____

_____

_____

_____

_____

_____

_____

_____

_____

What kind of reward system can I set up for myself as I achieve different milestones towards my goal?

By creating a clear plan of action, you'll be better equipped to overcome obstacles and stay on track towards achieving your desired outcomes. Don't forget to regularly track your progress and celebrate your successes along the way!

Setting achievable goals that are aligned with your desires and intentions will help you be better equipped to manifest your desired outcomes using the 369 method. This chapter will help you create a clear roadmap for success and stay motivated as you work towards your goals.

STEP3- RECOGNIZING LIMITING BELIEFS AND NEGATIVE THOUGHT PATTERNS

One of the biggest obstacles to successful manifestation is limiting beliefs and negative thought patterns. In this chapter, I will guide you to recognize these patterns and use techniques to challenge and reframe them, so you can overcome them and manifest your desired outcomes.

By recognizing and reframing limiting beliefs and negative thought patterns, you'll be better equipped to manifest your desired outcomes using the 369 method. This chapter will help you break free from self-doubt and negative self-talk, and cultivate a positive mindset that supports successful manifestation.

Guided Questions:

What are some beliefs that you have about yourself or your abilities that may be holding you back from achieving your goals?

_____

_____

_____

_____

_____

_____

_____

_____

_____

How have these limiting beliefs impacted your life so far?

_____

_____

_____

_____

_____

_____

_____

_____

_____

Where do you think these limiting beliefs come from? Are they based on past experiences or external influences?

_____

_____

_____

_____

_____

_____

_____

_____

_____

How would your life be different if you were able to let go of these limiting beliefs?

_____

_____

_____

_____

_____

_____

_____

_____

_____

What evidence do you have that these limiting beliefs are true? Is there any evidence that contradicts them?

What would happen if you chose to believe something different instead of these limiting beliefs?

How can you reframe these limiting beliefs in a more positive and empowering way?

What actions can you take to challenge these limiting beliefs and start making progress towards your goals?

Who can support you in challenging these limiting beliefs and holding you accountable for making positive changes?

_____

_____

_____

_____

_____

_____

_____

_____

_____

How will you know when you have successfully overcome these limiting beliefs and are making progress towards your desired outcomes?

_____

_____

_____

_____

_____

_____

_____

_____

_____

STEP 4- CREATING AFFIRMATIONS TO SUPPORT YOUR MANIFESTATIONS

Affirmations are powerful tools for manifestation as they help you focus your thoughts and beliefs on your desired outcomes. In this chapter, you will learn how to craft powerful and effective affirmations.

Guided Questions

What specific goal or outcome do you want to manifest in your life?

_____
_____
_____
_____
_____
_____
_____
_____
_____
_____

What limiting beliefs or negative self-talk do you need to overcome in order to achieve this goal?

_____
_____
_____
_____
_____
_____
_____
_____
_____
_____

What positive and empowering statements can you create to counteract those limiting beliefs and negative self-talk?

How can you make your affirmations specific and focused on the outcome you want to manifest?

How can you phrase your affirmations in a way that feels authentic and resonant with your true desires?

_____

_____

_____

_____

_____

_____

_____

_____

_____

What emotions or feelings do you want to evoke with your affirmations, and how can you choose words that help to create those emotions?

_____

_____

_____

_____

_____

_____

_____

_____

_____

How can you make your affirmations present-tense and affirmative, rather than negative or focused on what you don't want?

_____

_____

_____

_____

_____

_____

_____

_____

_____

How can you incorporate gratitude into your affirmations, and express gratitude for the outcome you want to manifest as if it has already happened?

_____

_____

_____

_____

_____

_____

_____

_____

_____

How often will you repeat your affirmations, and what methods will you use to integrate them into your daily practice?

_____

_____

_____

_____

_____

_____

_____

_____

_____

How can you track your progress and measure the effectiveness of your affirmations over time?

_____

_____

_____

_____

_____

_____

_____

_____

_____

SECTION 3

USING THE 369 METHOD

This section is where the rubber meets the road. Here, you'll find clear instructions and examples for using the 369 method, as well as space to write down your own affirmations and track your progress over time. This is where you'll put all of the tools and techniques you've learned in the previous sections into practice so you can manifest your desired outcomes.

To get started, find a quiet and comfortable space where you can focus your attention. Begin by setting a clear intention for what you want to manifest, and then follow these steps:

1. Write down your intention in a clear and concise statement, using positive and affirming language.

2. Write this statement down three times in the morning, six times in the afternoon, and nine times in the evening. Repeat this process every day for 21 days.

3. While writing your affirmations, visualize yourself already having achieved your desired outcome. Feel the emotions and sensations associated with this achievement.

4. As you write your affirmations, try to stay present and focused on the task at hand. Avoid distractions and negative self-talk.

In addition to practicing the 369 method, you can also track your progress over time. Use the pages provided in this section to write down your affirmations and practice the 369 method. Use the tools provided to track your progress and reflect on your experiences.

Remember that the 369 method is just one tool in your manifestation toolkit. Use it in conjunction with other techniques, such as meditation, visualization, and gratitude practices to enhance your manifestation practice.

By using this section to practice the 369 method, you'll be able to see tangible results and track your progress over time. This will help you stay motivated and focused, and enable you to refine and adapt your approach as needed. The ultimate goal of this section is to empower you to use the 369 method to manifest your desired outcomes with confidence and ease.

369 Manifestation Method

Date: ___/___/___

Write Your **Affirmation** 3 Times In The **Morning.**

_____

_____

_____

Write Your **Affirmation** 6 Times In The **Afternoon**.

_____

_____

_____

_____

_____

_____

Write Your **Affirmation** 9 Times In The **Evening.**

_____

_____

_____

_____

_____

_____

_____

_____

_____

369 Manifestation Method   Date: ___ / ___ / ___

Write Your **Affirmation** 3 Times In The **Morning.**

Write Your **Affirmation** 6 Times In The **Afternoon.**

Write Your **Affirmation** 9 Times In The **Evening.**

---

369 Manifestation Method   Date: __/__/__

Write Your **Affirmation** 3 Times In The **Morning.**

Write Your **Affirmation** 6 Times In The **Afternoon**.

Write Your **Affirmation** 9 Times In The **Evening.**

---

369 Manifestation Method   Date: ___/___/___

Write Your **Affirmation** 3 Times In The **Morning.**

Write Your **Affirmation** 6 Times In The **Afternoon.**

Write Your **Affirmation** 9 Times In The **Evening.**

----

369 Manifestation Method

Date: ___ / ___ /___

Write Your **Affirmation** 3 Times In The **Morning.**

_____
_____
_____

Write Your **Affirmation** 6 Times In The **Afternoon.**

_____
_____
_____
_____
_____

Write Your **Affirmation** 9 Times In The **Evening.**

_____
_____
_____
_____
_____
_____
_____
_____

369 Manifestation Method   Date: ___/___/___

Write Your **Affirmation** 3 Times In The **Morning.**

Write Your **Affirmation** 6 Times In The **Afternoon**.

Write Your **Affirmation** 9 Times In The **Evening.**

---

369 Manifestation Method

Date: ___/___/___

Write Your **Affirmation** 3 Times In The **Morning.**

_____
_____
_____

Write Your **Affirmation** 6 Times In The **Afternoon**.

_____
_____
_____
_____
_____
_____

Write Your **Affirmation** 9 Times In The **Evening.**

_____
_____
_____
_____
_____
_____
_____
_____
_____

369 Manifestation Method

Date: ___/___/___

Write Your **Affirmation** 3 Times In The **Morning.**

Write Your **Affirmation** 6 Times In The **Afternoon.**

Write Your **Affirmation** 9 Times In The **Evening.**

----

369 Manifestation Method   Date: ___/___/___

Write Your **Affirmation** 3 Times In The **Morning.**

Write Your **Affirmation** 6 Times In The **Afternoon**.

Write Your **Affirmation** 9 Times In The **Evening.**

----

369 Manifestation Method   Date: ___ / ___ /

Write Your **Affirmation** 3 Times In The **Morning.**

Write Your **Affirmation** 6 Times In The **Afternoon.**

Write Your **Affirmation** 9 Times In The **Evening.**

----

369 Manifestation Method   Date: ___/___/___

Write Your **Affirmation** 3 Times In The **Morning.**

Write Your **Affirmation** 6 Times In The **Afternoon**.

Write Your **Affirmation** 9 Times In The **Evening.**

---

369 Manifestation Method   Date: ___/___/___

Write Your **Affirmation** 3 Times In The **Morning.**

Write Your **Affirmation** 6 Times In The **Afternoon.**

Write Your **Affirmation** 9 Times In The **Evening.**

----

369 Manifestation Method   Date: __/__/__

☀ Write Your **Affirmation** 3 Times In The **Morning.**

🌅 Write Your **Affirmation** 6 Times In The **Afternoon.**

🌙 Write Your **Affirmation** 9 Times In The **Evening.**

---

369 Manifestation Method   Date: ___/___/

Write Your **Affirmation** 3 Times In The **Morning.**

_____

_____

Write Your **Affirmation** 6 Times In The **Afternoon**.

_____

_____

_____

_____

Write Your **Affirmation** 9 Times In The **Evening.**

_____

_____

_____

_____

_____

_____

369 Manifestation Method   Date: ___/___/___

Write Your **Affirmation** 3 Times In The **Morning.**

Write Your **Affirmation** 6 Times In The **Afternoon.**

Write Your **Affirmation** 9 Times In The **Evening.**

---

369 Manifestation Method   Date: __/__/__

Write Your **Affirmation** 3 Times In The **Morning.**

Write Your **Affirmation** 6 Times In The **Afternoon.**

Write Your **Affirmation** 9 Times In The **Evening.**

----

369 Manifestation Method

Date: ___/___/___

Write Your **Affirmation** 3 Times In The **Morning.**

Write Your **Affirmation** 6 Times In The **Afternoon**.

Write Your **Affirmation** 9 Times In The **Evening.**

---

369 Manifestation Method

Date: ___/___/___

Write Your **Affirmation** 3 Times In The **Morning.**

_____

_____

_____

Write Your **Affirmation** 6 Times In The **Afternoon**.

_____

_____

_____

_____

_____

_____

Write Your **Affirmation** 9 Times In The **Evening.**

_____

_____

_____

_____

_____

_____

_____

_____

_____

369 Manifestation Method

Date: ___/___/___

Write Your **Affirmation** 3 Times In The **Morning.**

Write Your **Affirmation** 6 Times In The **Afternoon**.

Write Your **Affirmation** 9 Times In The **Evening.**

----

369 Manifestation Method

Date: ___/___/___

Write Your **Affirmation** 3 Times In The **Morning.**

_____
_____
_____

Write Your **Affirmation** 6 Times In The **Afternoon.**

_____
_____
_____
_____
_____

Write Your **Affirmation** 9 Times In The **Evening.**

_____
_____
_____
_____
_____
_____
_____

369 Manifestation Method   Date: ___/___/___

Write Your **Affirmation** 3 Times In The **Morning.**

Write Your **Affirmation** 6 Times In The **Afternoon.**

Write Your **Affirmation** 9 Times In The **Evening.**

---

369 Manifestation Method   Date: __/__/__

Write Your **Affirmation** 3 Times In The **Morning.**

Write Your **Affirmation** 6 Times In The **Afternoon.**

Write Your **Affirmation** 9 Times In The **Evening.**

---

369 Manifestation Method   Date: ___/___/_

Write Your **Affirmation** 3 Times In The **Morning.**

Write Your **Affirmation** 6 Times In The **Afternoon**.

Write Your **Affirmation** 9 Times In The **Evening.**

----

369 Manifestation Method   Date: ___/___/__

Write Your **Affirmation** 3 Times In The **Morning.**

_____

_____

Write Your **Affirmation** 6 Times In The **Afternoon.**

_____

_____

_____

_____

Write Your **Affirmation** 9 Times In The **Evening.**

_____

_____

_____

_____

_____

_____

369 Manifestation Method

Date: ___/___/___

Write Your **Affirmation** 3 Times In The **Morning.**

Write Your **Affirmation** 6 Times In The **Afternoon**.

Write Your **Affirmation** 9 Times In The **Evening.**

---

369 Manifestation Method   Date: __/__/__

☀

Write Your **Affirmation** 3 Times In The **Morning.**

🌅

Write Your **Affirmation** 6 Times In The **Afternoon**.

🌙

Write Your **Affirmation** 9 Times In The **Evening.**

----

369 Manifestation Method

Date: ___/___/___

Write Your **Affirmation** 3 Times In The **Morning.**

_____

_____

_____

Write Your **Affirmation** 6 Times In The **Afternoon.**

_____

_____

_____

_____

_____

_____

Write Your **Affirmation** 9 Times In The **Evening.**

_____

_____

_____

_____

_____

_____

_____

_____

_____

369 Manifestation Method   Date: ___/___/

Write Your **Affirmation** 3 Times In The **Morning.**

Write Your **Affirmation** 6 Times In The **Afternoon**.

Write Your **Affirmation** 9 Times In The **Evening.**

----

369 Manifestation Method

Date: ___/___/___

Write Your **Affirmation** 3 Times In The **Morning.**

Write Your **Affirmation** 6 Times In The **Afternoon**.

Write Your **Affirmation** 9 Times In The **Evening.**

---

369 Manifestation Method   Date: ___/___/___

Write Your **Affirmation** 3 Times In The **Morning.**

_____

_____

Write Your **Affirmation** 6 Times In The **Afternoon.**

_____

_____

_____

_____

Write Your **Affirmation** 9 Times In The **Evening.**

_____

_____

_____

_____

_____

_____

369 Manifestation Method

Date: ___/___/___

☀️

Write Your **Affirmation** 3 Times In The **Morning.**

🌅

Write Your **Affirmation** 6 Times In The **Afternoon**.

🌙☁️

Write Your **Affirmation** 9 Times In The **Evening.**

---

369 Manifestation Method

Date: ___/___/__

Write Your **Affirmation** 3 Times In The **Morning.**

Write Your **Affirmation** 6 Times In The **Afternoon**.

Write Your **Affirmation** 9 Times In The **Evening.**

---

369 Manifestation Method

Date: ___/___/___

Write Your **Affirmation** 3 Times In The **Morning.**

Write Your **Affirmation** 6 Times In The **Afternoon.**

Write Your **Affirmation** 9 Times In The **Evening.**

----

369 Manifestation Method   Date: ___/___/___

Write Your **Affirmation** 3 Times In The **Morning.**

Write Your **Affirmation** 6 Times In The **Afternoon.**

Write Your **Affirmation** 9 Times In The **Evening.**

---

369 Manifestation Method

Date: ___/___/___

Write Your **Affirmation** 3 Times In The **Morning.**

Write Your **Affirmation** 6 Times In The **Afternoon.**

Write Your **Affirmation** 9 Times In The **Evening.**

---

369 Manifestation Method   Date: ___/___/___

Write Your **Affirmation** 3 Times In The **Morning.**

_____

_____

_____

Write Your **Affirmation** 6 Times In The **Afternoon.**

_____

_____

_____

_____

_____

_____

Write Your **Affirmation** 9 Times In The **Evening.**

_____

_____

_____

_____

_____

_____

_____

_____

_____

369 Manifestation Method

Date: ___/___/___

Write Your **Affirmation** 3 Times In The **Morning.**

Write Your **Affirmation** 6 Times In The **Afternoon.**

Write Your **Affirmation** 9 Times In The **Evening.**

----

369 Manifestation Method   Date: ___/___/___

Write Your **Affirmation** 3 Times In The **Morning.**

_____

_____

_____

Write Your **Affirmation** 6 Times In The **Afternoon.**

_____

_____

_____

_____

_____

_____

Write Your **Affirmation** 9 Times In The **Evening.**

_____

_____

_____

_____

_____

_____

_____

_____

_____

369 Manifestation Method   Date: ___/___/___

Write Your **Affirmation** 3 Times In The **Morning.**

Write Your **Affirmation** 6 Times In The **Afternoon.**

Write Your **Affirmation** 9 Times In The **Evening.**

----

369 Manifestation Method

Date: ___/___/___

Write Your **Affirmation** 3 Times In The **Morning.**

Write Your **Affirmation** 6 Times In The **Afternoon.**

Write Your **Affirmation** 9 Times In The **Evening.**

---

369 Manifestation Method   Date: ___/___/___

Write Your **Affirmation** 3 Times In The **Morning.**

Write Your **Affirmation** 6 Times In The **Afternoon**.

Write Your **Affirmation** 9 Times In The **Evening.**

---

369 Manifestation Method

Date: ___ / ___ / ___

Write Your **Affirmation** 3 Times In The **Morning.**

Write Your **Affirmation** 6 Times In The **Afternoon**.

Write Your **Affirmation** 9 Times In The **Evening.**

---

369 Manifestation Method

Date: ___/___/___

Write Your **Affirmation** 3 Times In The **Morning.**

Write Your **Affirmation** 6 Times In The **Afternoon.**

Write Your **Affirmation** 9 Times In The **Evening.**

---

369 Manifestation Method   Date: ___/___/___

Write Your **Affirmation** 3 Times In The **Morning.**

_____

_____

_____

Write Your **Affirmation** 6 Times In The **Afternoon.**

_____

_____

_____

_____

_____

Write Your **Affirmation** 9 Times In The **Evening.**

_____

_____

_____

_____

_____

_____

_____

369 Manifestation Method

Date: ___/___/___

Write Your **Affirmation** 3 Times In The **Morning.**

Write Your **Affirmation** 6 Times In The **Afternoon.**

Write Your **Affirmation** 9 Times In The **Evening.**

----

369 Manifestation Method   Date: ___/___/__

Write Your **Affirmation** 3 Times In The **Morning.**

_____

_____

_____

Write Your **Affirmation** 6 Times In The **Afternoon.**

_____

_____

_____

_____

_____

_____

Write Your **Affirmation** 9 Times In The **Evening.**

_____

_____

_____

_____

_____

_____

_____

_____

_____

369 Manifestation Method

Date: ___/___/___

Write Your **Affirmation** 3 Times In The **Morning.**

Write Your **Affirmation** 6 Times In The **Afternoon**.

Write Your **Affirmation** 9 Times In The **Evening.**

---

369 Manifestation Method   Date: ___/___/___

Write Your **Affirmation** 3 Times In The **Morning.**

_____

_____

_____

Write Your **Affirmation** 6 Times In The **Afternoon.**

_____

_____

_____

_____

_____

_____

Write Your **Affirmation** 9 Times In The **Evening.**

_____

_____

_____

_____

_____

_____

_____

_____

_____

369 Manifestation Method

Date: ___/___/__

Write Your **Affirmation** 3 Times In The **Morning.**

_____

_____

_____

Write Your **Affirmation** 6 Times In The **Afternoon**.

_____

_____

_____

_____

_____

_____

Write Your **Affirmation** 9 Times In The **Evening.**

_____

_____

_____

_____

_____

_____

_____

_____

_____

369 Manifestation Method   Date: ___/___/___

Write Your **Affirmation** 3 Times In The **Morning.**

_____
_____
_____

Write Your **Affirmation** 6 Times In The **Afternoon.**

_____
_____
_____
_____
_____
_____

Write Your **Affirmation** 9 Times In The **Evening.**

_____
_____
_____
_____
_____
_____
_____
_____
_____

369 Manifestation Method   Date: ___/___/___

Write Your **Affirmation** 3 Times In The **Morning.**

Write Your **Affirmation** 6 Times In The **Afternoon**.

Write Your **Affirmation** 9 Times In The **Evening.**

---

369 Manifestation Method Date: __/__/__

Write Your **Affirmation** 3 Times In The **Morning.**

Write Your **Affirmation** 6 Times In The **Afternoon**.

Write Your **Affirmation** 9 Times In The **Evening.**

---

369 Manifestation Method

Date: ___/___/___

Write Your **Affirmation** 3 Times In The **Morning.**

Write Your **Affirmation** 6 Times In The **Afternoon.**

Write Your **Affirmation** 9 Times In The **Evening.**

---

369 Manifestation Method

Date: ___/___/__

Write Your **Affirmation** 3 Times In The **Morning.**

_____

_____

_____

Write Your **Affirmation** 6 Times In The **Afternoon.**

_____

_____

_____

_____

_____

_____

Write Your **Affirmation** 9 Times In The **Evening.**

_____

_____

_____

_____

_____

_____

_____

_____

_____

369 Manifestation Method   Date: ___/___/__

Write Your **Affirmation** 3 Times In The **Morning.**

Write Your **Affirmation** 6 Times In The **Afternoon**.

Write Your **Affirmation** 9 Times In The **Evening.**

---

369 Manifestation Method   Date: __/__/__

Write Your **Affirmation** 3 Times In The **Morning.**

Write Your **Affirmation** 6 Times In The **Afternoon.**

Write Your **Affirmation** 9 Times In The **Evening.**

---

369 Manifestation Method   Date: ___/___/___

Write Your **Affirmation** 3 Times In The **Morning.**

Write Your **Affirmation** 6 Times In The **Afternoon**.

Write Your **Affirmation** 9 Times In The **Evening.**

----

369 Manifestation Method   Date: ___/___/___

Write Your **Affirmation** 3 Times In The **Morning.**

_____

_____

Write Your **Affirmation** 6 Times In The **Afternoon.**

_____

_____

_____

Write Your **Affirmation** 9 Times In The **Evening.**

_____

_____

_____

_____

_____

369 Manifestation Method

Date: ___/___/__

Write Your **Affirmation** 3 Times In The **Morning.**

Write Your **Affirmation** 6 Times In The **Afternoon.**

Write Your **Affirmation** 9 Times In The **Evening.**

----

369 Manifestation Method   Date: ___ / __ / __

Write Your **Affirmation** 3 Times In The **Morning.**

Write Your **Affirmation** 6 Times In The **Afternoon.**

Write Your **Affirmation** 9 Times In The **Evening.**

---

369 Manifestation Method

Date: ___/___/___

Write Your **Affirmation** 3 Times In The **Morning.**

Write Your **Affirmation** 6 Times In The **Afternoon.**

Write Your **Affirmation** 9 Times In The **Evening.**

----

369 Manifestation Method   Date: ___ / ___ / ___

Write Your **Affirmation** 3 Times In The **Morning.**

Write Your **Affirmation** 6 Times In The **Afternoon.**

Write Your **Affirmation** 9 Times In The **Evening.**

---

369 Manifestation Method

Date: ___/___/___

Write Your **Affirmation** 3 Times In The **Morning.**

_____

_____

_____

Write Your **Affirmation** 6 Times In The **Afternoon**.

_____

_____

_____

_____

_____

_____

Write Your **Affirmation** 9 Times In The **Evening.**

_____

_____

_____

_____

_____

_____

_____

_____

_____

369 Manifestation Method   Date: ___/___/___

Write Your **Affirmation** 3 Times In The **Morning.**

_____

_____

_____

Write Your **Affirmation** 6 Times In The **Afternoon.**

_____

_____

_____

_____

_____

_____

Write Your **Affirmation** 9 Times In The **Evening.**

_____

_____

_____

_____

_____

_____

_____

_____

_____

369 Manifestation Method   Date: ___/___/__

Write Your **Affirmation** 3 Times In The **Morning.**

Write Your **Affirmation** 6 Times In The **Afternoon.**

Write Your **Affirmation** 9 Times In The **Evening.**

---

369 Manifestation Method

Date: ___/___/___

Write Your **Affirmation** 3 Times In The **Morning.**

_____
_____
_____

Write Your **Affirmation** 6 Times In The **Afternoon.**

_____
_____
_____
_____
_____
_____

Write Your **Affirmation** 9 Times In The **Evening.**

_____
_____
_____
_____
_____
_____
_____
_____
_____

369 Manifestation Method

Date: ___/___/___

Write Your **Affirmation** 3 Times In The **Morning.**

Write Your **Affirmation** 6 Times In The **Afternoon**.

Write Your **Affirmation** 9 Times In The **Evening.**

---

369 Manifestation Method   Date: ___/___/__

Write Your **Affirmation** 3 Times In The **Morning.**

Write Your **Affirmation** 6 Times In The **Afternoon.**

Write Your **Affirmation** 9 Times In The **Evening.**

---

369 Manifestation Method

Date: ___/___/___

Write Your **Affirmation** 3 Times In The **Morning.**

Write Your **Affirmation** 6 Times In The **Afternoon.**

Write Your **Affirmation** 9 Times In The **Evening.**

---

369 Manifestation Method   Date: ___/___/___

Write Your **Affirmation** 3 Times In The **Morning.**

_____

_____

_____

Write Your **Affirmation** 6 Times In The **Afternoon.**

_____

_____

_____

_____

_____

Write Your **Affirmation** 9 Times In The **Evening.**

_____

_____

_____

_____

_____

_____

_____

_____

369 Manifestation Method

Date: ___/___/___

Write Your **Affirmation** 3 Times In The **Morning.**

_____
_____
_____

Write Your **Affirmation** 6 Times In The **Afternoon.**

_____
_____
_____
_____
_____
_____

Write Your **Affirmation** 9 Times In The **Evening.**

_____
_____
_____
_____
_____
_____
_____
_____
_____

369 Manifestation Method   Date: __/__/__

Write Your **Affirmation** 3 Times In The **Morning.**

_____

_____

_____

Write Your **Affirmation** 6 Times In The **Afternoon.**

_____

_____

_____

_____

_____

_____

Write Your **Affirmation** 9 Times In The **Evening.**

_____

_____

_____

_____

_____

_____

_____

_____

_____

369 Manifestation Method   Date: __/__/_

Write Your **Affirmation** 3 Times In The **Morning.**

Write Your **Affirmation** 6 Times In The **Afternoon**.

Write Your **Affirmation** 9 Times In The **Evening.**

---

369 Manifestation Method   Date: ___/___/___

Write Your **Affirmation** 3 Times In The **Morning.**

Write Your **Affirmation** 6 Times In The **Afternoon.**

Write Your **Affirmation** 9 Times In The **Evening.**

---

369 Manifestation Method

Date: __/__/__

Write Your **Affirmation** 3 Times In The **Morning.**

_____
_____
_____

Write Your **Affirmation** 6 Times In The **Afternoon**.

_____
_____
_____
_____
_____
_____

Write Your **Affirmation** 9 Times In The **Evening.**

_____
_____
_____
_____
_____
_____
_____
_____
_____

369 Manifestation Method

Date: ___/___/___

Write Your **Affirmation** 3 Times In The **Morning.**

_____

_____

_____

Write Your **Affirmation** 6 Times In The **Afternoon.**

_____

_____

_____

_____

Write Your **Affirmation** 9 Times In The **Evening.**

_____

_____

_____

_____

_____

_____

_____

369 Manifestation Method   Date: ___/___/___

Write Your **Affirmation** 3 Times In The **Morning.**

_____

_____

_____

Write Your **Affirmation** 6 Times In The **Afternoon**.

_____

_____

_____

_____

_____

_____

Write Your **Affirmation** 9 Times In The **Evening.**

_____

_____

_____

_____

_____

_____

_____

_____

_____

369 Manifestation Method   Date: ___/___/___

☀️

Write Your **Affirmation** 3 Times In The **Morning.**

_____
_____
_____

🌅

Write Your **Affirmation** 6 Times In The **Afternoon.**

_____
_____
_____
_____

🌙

Write Your **Affirmation** 9 Times In The **Evening.**

_____
_____
_____
_____
_____
_____
_____

369 Manifestation Method   Date: ___/___/___

Write Your **Affirmation** 3 Times In The **Morning.**

Write Your **Affirmation** 6 Times In The **Afternoon.**

Write Your **Affirmation** 9 Times In The **Evening.**

---

369 Manifestation Method   Date: ___/___/___

Write Your **Affirmation** 3 Times In The **Morning.**

Write Your **Affirmation** 6 Times In The **Afternoon.**

Write Your **Affirmation** 9 Times In The **Evening.**

---

369 Manifestation Method   Date: ___/___/___

Write Your **Affirmation** 3 Times In The **Morning.**

Write Your **Affirmation** 6 Times In The **Afternoon**.

Write Your **Affirmation** 9 Times In The **Evening.**

---

369 Manifestation Method

Date: ___/___/___

Write Your **Affirmation** 3 Times In The **Morning.**

Write Your **Affirmation** 6 Times In The **Afternoon.**

Write Your **Affirmation** 9 Times In The **Evening.**

----

369 Manifestation Method   Date: ___/___/___

Write Your **Affirmation** 3 Times In The **Morning.**

_____
_____
_____

Write Your **Affirmation** 6 Times In The **Afternoon.**

_____
_____
_____
_____
_____
_____

Write Your **Affirmation** 9 Times In The **Evening.**

_____
_____
_____
_____
_____
_____
_____
_____
_____

369 Manifestation Method   Date: ___/___/___

Write Your **Affirmation** 3 Times In The **Morning.**

Write Your **Affirmation** 6 Times In The **Afternoon.**

Write Your **Affirmation** 9 Times In The **Evening.**

----

369 Manifestation Method   Date: ___/___/___

Write Your **Affirmation** 3 Times In The **Morning.**

Write Your **Affirmation** 6 Times In The **Afternoon**.

Write Your **Affirmation** 9 Times In The **Evening.**

----

369 Manifestation Method Date: __/__/__

Write Your **Affirmation** 3 Times In The **Morning.**

Write Your **Affirmation** 6 Times In The **Afternoon.**

Write Your **Affirmation** 9 Times In The **Evening.**

---

369 Manifestation Method   Date: ___/___/___

Write Your **Affirmation** 3 Times In The **Morning.**

Write Your **Affirmation** 6 Times In The **Afternoon**.

Write Your **Affirmation** 9 Times In The **Evening.**

----

369 Manifestation Method   Date: ___/___/___

Write Your **Affirmation** 3 Times In The **Morning.**

Write Your **Affirmation** 6 Times In The **Afternoon.**

Write Your **Affirmation** 9 Times In The **Evening.**

---

369 Manifestation Method

Date: ___/___/___

Write Your **Affirmation** 3 Times In The **Morning.**

Write Your **Affirmation** 6 Times In The **Afternoon**.

Write Your **Affirmation** 9 Times In The **Evening.**

---

369 Manifestation Method

Date: ___/___/___

Write Your **Affirmation** 3 Times In The **Morning.**

_____

_____

_____

Write Your **Affirmation** 6 Times In The **Afternoon.**

_____

_____

_____

_____

Write Your **Affirmation** 9 Times In The **Evening.**

_____

_____

_____

_____

_____

_____

_____

369 Manifestation Method   Date: ___/___/___

Write Your **Affirmation** 3 Times In The **Morning.**

Write Your **Affirmation** 6 Times In The **Afternoon**.

Write Your **Affirmation** 9 Times In The **Evening.**

---

369 Manifestation Method   Date: ___/___/___

Write Your **Affirmation** 3 Times In The **Morning.**

Write Your **Affirmation** 6 Times In The **Afternoon**.

Write Your **Affirmation** 9 Times In The **Evening.**

---

369 Manifestation Method

Date: ___/___/___

Write Your **Affirmation** 3 Times In The **Morning.**

_____
_____
_____

Write Your **Affirmation** 6 Times In The **Afternoon**.

_____
_____
_____
_____
_____
_____

Write Your **Affirmation** 9 Times In The **Evening.**

_____
_____
_____
_____
_____
_____
_____
_____
_____

369 Manifestation Method

Date: ___/___/___

Write Your **Affirmation** 3 Times In The **Morning.**

Write Your **Affirmation** 6 Times In The **Afternoon.**

Write Your **Affirmation** 9 Times In The **Evening.**

----

369 Manifestation Method   Date: ___/___/___

Write Your **Affirmation** 3 Times In The **Morning.**

Write Your **Affirmation** 6 Times In The **Afternoon**.

Write Your **Affirmation** 9 Times In The **Evening.**

---

369 Manifestation Method   Date: ___/___/__

Write Your **Affirmation** 3 Times In The **Morning.**

Write Your **Affirmation** 6 Times In The **Afternoon.**

Write Your **Affirmation** 9 Times In The **Evening.**

---

369 Manifestation Method

Date: ___/___/___

Write Your **Affirmation** 3 Times In The **Morning.**

Write Your **Affirmation** 6 Times In The **Afternoon**.

Write Your **Affirmation** 9 Times In The **Evening.**

369 Manifestation Method

Date: ___/___/___

Write Your **Affirmation** 3 Times In The **Morning.**

Write Your **Affirmation** 6 Times In The **Afternoon.**

Write Your **Affirmation** 9 Times In The **Evening.**

----

369 Manifestation Method   Date: ___/___/___

Write Your **Affirmation** 3 Times In The **Morning.**

Write Your **Affirmation** 6 Times In The **Afternoon**.

Write Your **Affirmation** 9 Times In The **Evening.**

----

369 Manifestation Method

Date: ___/___/___

Write Your **Affirmation** 3 Times In The **Morning.**

Write Your **Affirmation** 6 Times In The **Afternoon.**

Write Your **Affirmation** 9 Times In The **Evening.**

---

369 Manifestation Method

Date: ___/___/___

Write Your **Affirmation** 3 Times In The **Morning.**

Write Your **Affirmation** 6 Times In The **Afternoon.**

Write Your **Affirmation** 9 Times In The **Evening.**

---

369 Manifestation Method

Date: ___/___/___

Write Your **Affirmation** 3 Times In The **Morning.**

Write Your **Affirmation** 6 Times In The **Afternoon.**

Write Your **Affirmation** 9 Times In The **Evening.**

---

369 Manifestation Method   Date: ___/___/___

Write Your **Affirmation** 3 Times In The **Morning.**

Write Your **Affirmation** 6 Times In The **Afternoon**.

Write Your **Affirmation** 9 Times In The **Evening.**

----

369 Manifestation Method   Date: ___/___/___

Write Your **Affirmation** 3 Times In The **Morning.**

Write Your **Affirmation** 6 Times In The **Afternoon.**

Write Your **Affirmation** 9 Times In The **Evening.**

----

369 Manifestation Method   Date: ___/___/___

Write Your **Affirmation** 3 Times In The **Morning.**

Write Your **Affirmation** 6 Times In The **Afternoon.**

Write Your **Affirmation** 9 Times In The **Evening.**

---

369 Manifestation Method

Date: ___/___/___

Write Your **Affirmation** 3 Times In The **Morning.**

Write Your **Affirmation** 6 Times In The **Afternoon**.

Write Your **Affirmation** 9 Times In The **Evening.**

----

369 Manifestation Method   Date: __/__/__

Write Your **Affirmation** 3 Times In The **Morning.**

Write Your **Affirmation** 6 Times In The **Afternoon.**

Write Your **Affirmation** 9 Times In The **Evening.**

---

369 Manifestation Method

Date: ___/___/___

Write Your **Affirmation** 3 Times In The **Morning.**

Write Your **Affirmation** 6 Times In The **Afternoon.**

Write Your **Affirmation** 9 Times In The **Evening.**

---

369 Manifestation Method   Date: __/__/__

Write Your **Affirmation** 3 Times In The **Morning.**

Write Your **Affirmation** 6 Times In The **Afternoon.**

Write Your **Affirmation** 9 Times In The **Evening.**

----

369 Manifestation Method   Date: ___/___/___

Write Your **Affirmation** 3 Times In The **Morning.**

_____

_____

_____

Write Your **Affirmation** 6 Times In The **Afternoon.**

_____

_____

_____

_____

Write Your **Affirmation** 9 Times In The **Evening.**

_____

_____

_____

_____

_____

_____

_____

369 Manifestation Method   Date: ___/___/___

Write Your **Affirmation** 3 Times In The **Morning.**

Write Your **Affirmation** 6 Times In The **Afternoon.**

Write Your **Affirmation** 9 Times In The **Evening.**

----

369 Manifestation Method

Date: ___/___/___

Write Your **Affirmation** 3 Times In The **Morning.**

_____

_____

_____

Write Your **Affirmation** 6 Times In The **Afternoon.**

_____

_____

_____

_____

Write Your **Affirmation** 9 Times In The **Evening.**

_____

_____

_____

_____

_____

_____

_____

369 Manifestation Method

Date: __/__/__

Write Your **Affirmation** 3 Times In The **Morning.**

Write Your **Affirmation** 6 Times In The **Afternoon.**

Write Your **Affirmation** 9 Times In The **Evening.**

---

369 Manifestation Method

Date: ___/___/___

Write Your **Affirmation** 3 Times In The **Morning.**

Write Your **Affirmation** 6 Times In The **Afternoon.**

Write Your **Affirmation** 9 Times In The **Evening.**

---

369 Manifestation Method

Date: ___/___/___

Write Your **Affirmation** 3 Times In The **Morning.**

_____

_____

_____

Write Your **Affirmation** 6 Times In The **Afternoon**.

_____

_____

_____

_____

_____

_____

Write Your **Affirmation** 9 Times In The **Evening.**

_____

_____

_____

_____

_____

_____

_____

_____

_____

369 Manifestation Method   Date: ___/___/___

Write Your **Affirmation** 3 Times In The **Morning.**

Write Your **Affirmation** 6 Times In The **Afternoon.**

Write Your **Affirmation** 9 Times In The **Evening.**

----

369 Manifestation Method   Date: ___/___/___

Write Your **Affirmation** 3 Times In The **Morning.**

Write Your **Affirmation** 6 Times In The **Afternoon**.

Write Your **Affirmation** 9 Times In The **Evening.**

----

369 Manifestation Method   Date: ___/___/___

Write Your **Affirmation** 3 Times In The **Morning.**

Write Your **Affirmation** 6 Times In The **Afternoon.**

Write Your **Affirmation** 9 Times In The **Evening.**

----

369 Manifestation Method   Date: __/__/__

Write Your **Affirmation** 3 Times In The **Morning.**

Write Your **Affirmation** 6 Times In The **Afternoon.**

Write Your **Affirmation** 9 Times In The **Evening.**

---

369 Manifestation Method   Date: ___/___/__

Write Your **Affirmation** 3 Times In The **Morning.**

Write Your **Affirmation** 6 Times In The **Afternoon.**

Write Your **Affirmation** 9 Times In The **Evening.**

---

369 Manifestation Method

Date: ___/___/___

Write Your **Affirmation** 3 Times In The **Morning.**

Write Your **Affirmation** 6 Times In The **Afternoon**.

Write Your **Affirmation** 9 Times In The **Evening**.

---

369 Manifestation Method   Date: ___/___/___

Write Your **Affirmation** 3 Times In The **Morning.**

_____

_____

_____

Write Your **Affirmation** 6 Times In The **Afternoon.**

_____

_____

_____

_____

_____

_____

Write Your **Affirmation** 9 Times In The **Evening.**

_____

_____

_____

_____

_____

_____

_____

_____

_____

369 Manifestation Method   Date: ___/___/___

Write Your **Affirmation** 3 Times In The **Morning.**

_____

Write Your **Affirmation** 6 Times In The **Afternoon**.

_____

Write Your **Affirmation** 9 Times In The **Evening.**

_____

369 Manifestation Method

Date: ___/___/___

Write Your **Affirmation** 3 Times In The **Morning.**

Write Your **Affirmation** 6 Times In The **Afternoon.**

Write Your **Affirmation** 9 Times In The **Evening.**

181

369 Manifestation Method   Date: __/__/__

Write Your **Affirmation** 3 Times In The **Morning.**

Write Your **Affirmation** 6 Times In The **Afternoon.**

Write Your **Affirmation** 9 Times In The **Evening.**

---

369 Manifestation Method

Date: ___/___/___

Write Your **Affirmation** 3 Times In The **Morning.**

Write Your **Affirmation** 6 Times In The **Afternoon.**

Write Your **Affirmation** 9 Times In The **Evening.**

---

369 Manifestation Method

Date: ___/___/___

Write Your **Affirmation** 3 Times In The **Morning.**

Write Your **Affirmation** 6 Times In The **Afternoon.**

Write Your **Affirmation** 9 Times In The **Evening.**

---

369 Manifestation Method

Date: ___/___/___

Write Your **Affirmation** 3 Times In The **Morning.**

_____
_____
_____

Write Your **Affirmation** 6 Times In The **Afternoon.**

_____
_____
_____
_____

Write Your **Affirmation** 9 Times In The **Evening.**

_____
_____
_____
_____
_____
_____

369 Manifestation Method

Date: ___/___/___

Write Your **Affirmation** 3 Times In The **Morning.**

Write Your **Affirmation** 6 Times In The **Afternoon**.

Write Your **Affirmation** 9 Times In The **Evening.**

---

369 Manifestation Method   Date: __/__/__

Write Your **Affirmation** 3 Times In The **Morning.**

Write Your **Affirmation** 6 Times In The **Afternoon**.

Write Your **Affirmation** 9 Times In The **Evening.**

----

369 Manifestation Method   Date: ___/___/___

Write Your **Affirmation** 3 Times In The **Morning.**

_____
_____
_____

Write Your **Affirmation** 6 Times In The **Afternoon.**

_____
_____
_____
_____
_____
_____

Write Your **Affirmation** 9 Times In The **Evening.**

_____
_____
_____
_____
_____
_____
_____
_____
_____

369 Manifestation Method   Date: ___/___/___

Write Your **Affirmation** 3 Times In The **Morning.**

Write Your **Affirmation** 6 Times In The **Afternoon.**

Write Your **Affirmation** 9 Times In The **Evening.**

---

369 Manifestation Method   Date: ___/___/___

Write Your **Affirmation** 3 Times In The **Morning.**

Write Your **Affirmation** 6 Times In The **Afternoon**.

Write Your **Affirmation** 9 Times In The **Evening.**

----

369 Manifestation Method   Date: ___/___/___

Write Your **Affirmation** 3 Times In The **Morning.**

Write Your **Affirmation** 6 Times In The **Afternoon.**

Write Your **Affirmation** 9 Times In The **Evening.**

----

369 Manifestation Method   Date: __/__/__

Write Your **Affirmation** 3 Times In The **Morning.**

_____
_____
_____

Write Your **Affirmation** 6 Times In The **Afternoon**.

_____
_____
_____
_____
_____
_____

Write Your **Affirmation** 9 Times In The **Evening.**

_____
_____
_____
_____
_____
_____
_____
_____
_____

369 Manifestation Method   Date: ___/___/___

Write Your **Affirmation** 3 Times In The **Morning.**

Write Your **Affirmation** 6 Times In The **Afternoon.**

Write Your **Affirmation** 9 Times In The **Evening.**

----

369 Manifestation Method

Date: ___/___/___

Write Your **Affirmation** 3 Times In The **Morning.**

Write Your **Affirmation** 6 Times In The **Afternoon**.

Write Your **Affirmation** 9 Times In The **Evening.**

369 Manifestation Method

Date: ___/___/___

Write Your **Affirmation** 3 Times In The **Morning.**

_____

_____

_____

Write Your **Affirmation** 6 Times In The **Afternoon.**

_____

_____

_____

_____

_____

_____

Write Your **Affirmation** 9 Times In The **Evening.**

_____

_____

_____

_____

_____

_____

_____

_____

_____

369 Manifestation Method

Date: ___/___/___

Write Your **Affirmation** 3 Times In The **Morning.**

_____

_____

_____

Write Your **Affirmation** 6 Times In The **Afternoon**.

_____

_____

_____

_____

_____

_____

Write Your **Affirmation** 9 Times In The **Evening.**

_____

_____

_____

_____

_____

_____

_____

_____

_____

369 Manifestation Method   Date: ___/___/___

Write Your **Affirmation** 3 Times In The **Morning.**

_____

_____

_____

Write Your **Affirmation** 6 Times In The **Afternoon.**

_____

_____

_____

_____

_____

Write Your **Affirmation** 9 Times In The **Evening.**

_____

_____

_____

_____

_____

_____

_____

_____

_____

369 Manifestation Method   Date: ___/___/___

Write Your **Affirmation** 3 Times In The **Morning.**

_____
_____
_____

Write Your **Affirmation** 6 Times In The **Afternoon.**

_____
_____
_____
_____
_____
_____

Write Your **Affirmation** 9 Times In The **Evening.**

_____
_____
_____
_____
_____
_____
_____
_____
_____

369 Manifestation Method   Date: ___/___/___

Write Your **Affirmation** 3 Times In The **Morning.**

Write Your **Affirmation** 6 Times In The **Afternoon.**

Write Your **Affirmation** 9 Times In The **Evening.**

---

369 Manifestation Method   Date: ___/___/___

Write Your **Affirmation** 3 Times In The **Morning.**

Write Your **Affirmation** 6 Times In The **Afternoon.**

Write Your **Affirmation** 9 Times In The **Evening.**

---

369 Manifestation Method   Date: __/__/__

Write Your **Affirmation** 3 Times In The **Morning.**

Write Your **Affirmation** 6 Times In The **Afternoon.**

Write Your **Affirmation** 9 Times In The **Evening.**

---

369 Manifestation Method   Date: ___/___/___

Write Your **Affirmation** 3 Times In The **Morning.**

Write Your **Affirmation** 6 Times In The **Afternoon**.

Write Your **Affirmation** 9 Times In The **Evening.**

---

369 Manifestation Method

Date: ___/___/___

Write Your **Affirmation** 3 Times In The **Morning.**

Write Your **Affirmation** 6 Times In The **Afternoon.**

Write Your **Affirmation** 9 Times In The **Evening.**

----

369 Manifestation Method   Date: ___/___/___

Write Your **Affirmation** 3 Times In The **Morning.**

_____
_____
_____

Write Your **Affirmation** 6 Times In The **Afternoon.**

_____
_____
_____
_____
_____
_____

Write Your **Affirmation** 9 Times In The **Evening.**

_____
_____
_____
_____
_____
_____
_____
_____
_____

369 Manifestation Method

Date: ___/___/___

Write Your **Affirmation** 3 Times In The **Morning.**

_____

_____

_____

Write Your **Affirmation** 6 Times In The **Afternoon.**

_____

_____

_____

_____

_____

Write Your **Affirmation** 9 Times In The **Evening.**

_____

_____

_____

_____

_____

_____

_____

369 Manifestation Method   Date: __/__/__

Write Your **Affirmation** 3 Times In The **Morning.**

_____

_____

_____

Write Your **Affirmation** 6 Times In The **Afternoon.**

_____

_____

_____

_____

_____

_____

Write Your **Affirmation** 9 Times In The **Evening.**

_____

_____

_____

_____

_____

_____

_____

_____

_____

369 Manifestation Method   Date: __/__/__

Write Your **Affirmation** 3 Times In The **Morning.**

Write Your **Affirmation** 6 Times In The **Afternoon.**

Write Your **Affirmation** 9 Times In The **Evening.**

----

369 Manifestation Method

Date: ___/___/___

Write Your **Affirmation** 3 Times In The **Morning.**

Write Your **Affirmation** 6 Times In The **Afternoon.**

Write Your **Affirmation** 9 Times In The **Evening.**

----

369 Manifestation Method   Date: __/__/__

Write Your **Affirmation** 3 Times In The **Morning.**

Write Your **Affirmation** 6 Times In The **Afternoon.**

Write Your **Affirmation** 9 Times In The **Evening.**

---

369 Manifestation Method

Date: ___/___/___

Write Your **Affirmation** 3 Times In The **Morning.**

_____
_____
_____

Write Your **Affirmation** 6 Times In The **Afternoon.**

_____
_____
_____
_____
_____
_____

Write Your **Affirmation** 9 Times In The **Evening.**

_____
_____
_____
_____
_____
_____
_____
_____
_____

369 Manifestation Method   Date: ___/___/___.

Write Your **Affirmation** 3 Times In The **Morning.**

Write Your **Affirmation** 6 Times In The **Afternoon.**

Write Your **Affirmation** 9 Times In The **Evening.**

----

369 Manifestation Method   Date: __/__/__

Write Your **Affirmation** 3 Times In The **Morning.**

Write Your **Affirmation** 6 Times In The **Afternoon**.

Write Your **Affirmation** 9 Times In The **Evening.**

---

369 Manifestation Method

Date: ___/___/___

Write Your **Affirmation** 3 Times In The **Morning.**

Write Your **Affirmation** 6 Times In The **Afternoon.**

Write Your **Affirmation** 9 Times In The **Evening.**

---

369 Manifestation Method

Date: __/__/__

Write Your **Affirmation** 3 Times In The **Morning.**

Write Your **Affirmation** 6 Times In The **Afternoon**.

Write Your **Affirmation** 9 Times In The **Evening.**

----

369 Manifestation Method   Date: ___/___/_

Write Your **Affirmation** 3 Times In The **Morning.**

Write Your **Affirmation** 6 Times In The **Afternoon.**

Write Your **Affirmation** 9 Times In The **Evening.**

369 Manifestation Method Date: ___/___/___

Write Your **Affirmation** 3 Times In The **Morning.**

_____

_____

_____

Write Your **Affirmation** 6 Times In The **Afternoon.**

_____

_____

_____

_____

_____

_____

Write Your **Affirmation** 9 Times In The **Evening.**

_____

_____

_____

_____

_____

_____

_____

_____

_____

369 Manifestation Method   Date: ___/___/___

Write Your **Affirmation** 3 Times In The **Morning.**

Write Your **Affirmation** 6 Times In The **Afternoon.**

Write Your **Affirmation** 9 Times In The **Evening.**

---

369 Manifestation Method   Date: ___/___/___

Write Your **Affirmation** 3 Times In The **Morning.**

_____

_____

_____

Write Your **Affirmation** 6 Times In The **Afternoon.**

_____

_____

_____

_____

_____

_____

Write Your **Affirmation** 9 Times In The **Evening.**

_____

_____

_____

_____

_____

_____

_____

_____

_____

369 Manifestation Method

Date: ___/___/___

Write Your **Affirmation** 3 Times In The **Morning.**

Write Your **Affirmation** 6 Times In The **Afternoon.**

Write Your **Affirmation** 9 Times In The **Evening.**

---

369 Manifestation Method   Date: ___/___/___

Write Your **Affirmation** 3 Times In The **Morning.**

Write Your **Affirmation** 6 Times In The **Afternoon**.

Write Your **Affirmation** 9 Times In The **Evening.**

---

369 Manifestation Method   Date: ___/___/__

Write Your **Affirmation** 3 Times In The **Morning.**

Write Your **Affirmation** 6 Times In The **Afternoon.**

Write Your **Affirmation** 9 Times In The **Evening.**

---

369 Manifestation Method   Date: ___/___/__

Write Your **Affirmation** 3 Times In The **Morning.**

_____

_____

Write Your **Affirmation** 6 Times In The **Afternoon.**

_____

_____

_____

_____

Write Your **Affirmation** 9 Times In The **Evening.**

_____

_____

_____

_____

_____

_____

369 Manifestation Method

Date: ___/___/___

Write Your **Affirmation** 3 Times In The **Morning.**

_____

_____

_____

Write Your **Affirmation** 6 Times In The **Afternoon.**

_____

_____

_____

_____

Write Your **Affirmation** 9 Times In The **Evening.**

_____

_____

_____

_____

_____

_____

369 Manifestation Method   Date: __/__/__

Write Your **Affirmation** 3 Times In The **Morning.**

Write Your **Affirmation** 6 Times In The **Afternoon.**

Write Your **Affirmation** 9 Times In The **Evening.**

----

369 Manifestation Method   Date: ___/___/__

Write Your **Affirmation** 3 Times In The **Morning.**

Write Your **Affirmation** 6 Times In The **Afternoon.**

Write Your **Affirmation** 9 Times In The **Evening.**

---

369 Manifestation Method   Date: ___/___/__

Write Your **Affirmation** 3 Times In The **Morning.**

Write Your **Affirmation** 6 Times In The **Afternoon.**

Write Your **Affirmation** 9 Times In The **Evening.**

---

369 Manifestation Method   Date: ___/___/___

Write Your **Affirmation** 3 Times In The **Morning.**

_____

_____

_____

Write Your **Affirmation** 6 Times In The **Afternoon.**

_____

_____

_____

_____

_____

_____

Write Your **Affirmation** 9 Times In The **Evening.**

_____

_____

_____

_____

_____

_____

_____

_____

_____

369 Manifestation Method

Date: ___/___/___

Write Your **Affirmation** 3 Times In The **Morning.**

_____

_____

_____

Write Your **Affirmation** 6 Times In The **Afternoon.**

_____

_____

_____

_____

_____

_____

Write Your **Affirmation** 9 Times In The **Evening.**

_____

_____

_____

_____

_____

_____

_____

_____

_____

369 Manifestation Method

Date: ___/___/___

Write Your **Affirmation** 3 Times In The **Morning.**

Write Your **Affirmation** 6 Times In The **Afternoon.**

Write Your **Affirmation** 9 Times In The **Evening.**

---

369 Manifestation Method   Date: __/__/__

Write Your **Affirmation** 3 Times In The **Morning.**

Write Your **Affirmation** 6 Times In The **Afternoon.**

Write Your **Affirmation** 9 Times In The **Evening.**

----

369 Manifestation Method

Date: ___/___/___

Write Your **Affirmation** 3 Times In The **Morning.**

Write Your **Affirmation** 6 Times In The **Afternoon.**

Write Your **Affirmation** 9 Times In The **Evening.**

---

369 Manifestation Method

Date: ___/___/___

Write Your **Affirmation** 3 Times In The **Morning.**

Write Your **Affirmation** 6 Times In The **Afternoon**.

Write Your **Affirmation** 9 Times In The **Evening.**

----

369 Manifestation Method   Date: ___/___/___

Write Your **Affirmation** 3 Times In The **Morning.**

Write Your **Affirmation** 6 Times In The **Afternoon.**

Write Your **Affirmation** 9 Times In The **Evening.**

----

369 Manifestation Method   Date: __/__/__

Write Your **Affirmation** 3 Times In The **Morning.**

Write Your **Affirmation** 6 Times In The **Afternoon.**

Write Your **Affirmation** 9 Times In The **Evening.**

----

369 Manifestation Method

Date: ___/___/___

Write Your **Affirmation** 3 Times In The **Morning.**

_____

_____

_____

Write Your **Affirmation** 6 Times In The **Afternoon.**

_____

_____

_____

_____

_____

_____

Write Your **Affirmation** 9 Times In The **Evening.**

_____

_____

_____

_____

_____

_____

_____

_____

_____

369 Manifestation Method

Date: __/__/__

Write Your **Affirmation** 3 Times In The **Morning.**

_____

_____

_____

Write Your **Affirmation** 6 Times In The **Afternoon.**

_____

_____

_____

_____

_____

_____

Write Your **Affirmation** 9 Times In The **Evening.**

_____

_____

_____

_____

_____

_____

_____

_____

_____

369 Manifestation Method

Date: ___/___/___

Write Your **Affirmation** 3 Times In The **Morning.**

_____

_____

_____

Write Your **Affirmation** 6 Times In The **Afternoon.**

_____

_____

_____

_____

_____

_____

Write Your **Affirmation** 9 Times In The **Evening.**

_____

_____

_____

_____

_____

_____

_____

_____

_____

SECTION 4

ENHANCING YOUR MANIFESTATION PRACTICE

To truly master the art of manifestation, it's important to incorporate a variety of practices and techniques into your daily routine. In this section, you'll discover additional tools for enhancing your manifestation practice and attracting your desired outcomes with greater ease.

Meditation and Visualization Exercises

Meditation and visualization are powerful techniques for calming the mind, focusing your intentions, and raising your vibration to attract positive energy. You'll find exercises and techniques for incorporating meditation and visualization into your manifestation practice.

Gratitude and Appreciation Practices

Gratitude and appreciation are key to attracting abundance and positivity into your life. You'll discover practices and exercises for cultivating gratitude and appreciation in your daily life, which can help to shift your mindset and increase your vibration.

Self-Care and Self-Love Practices

Self-care and self-love practices are essential for supporting your overall well-being and helping you to manifest your desired outcomes. You'll learn techniques for taking care of yourself and loving yourself, including journaling, self-reflection, and self-compassion exercises.

By incorporating these additional tools and techniques into your manifestation practice, you'll be better equipped to align your thoughts, emotions, and actions with your desired outcomes and attract abundance and positivity into your life with greater ease.

Guided Questions

How can you incorporate meditation into your manifestation practice?

_____

_____

_____

_____

_____

_____

_____

_____

_____

_____

What visualization exercises resonate with you and your desired outcomes?

_____

_____

_____

_____

_____

_____

_____

_____

_____

_____

How can you cultivate a daily gratitude practice to enhance your manifestation process?

What self-care and self-love practices can you prioritize to support your overall well-being and manifestation practice?

How can you use these additional tools and techniques to deepen your connection to your desires and intentions?

SECTION 5

TROUBLESHOOTING YOUR MANIFESTATION PRACTICE

While manifestation can be a powerful tool for achieving your goals and desires, it's not always a smooth and easy process. In this section, we'll explore common challenges and obstacles that people encounter when trying to manifest their desires. We'll also provide strategies for overcoming resistance and doubt, and staying motivated and consistent with your practice.

Common Challenges and Obstacles to Manifestation

One of the biggest challenges people face when trying to manifest their desires is self-doubt. It's easy to get caught up in negative self-talk and limiting beliefs that can sabotage your efforts. Other common obstacles include fear, lack of clarity, and difficulty staying focused and motivated.

Strategies for Overcoming Resistance and Doubt

The first step in overcoming resistance and doubt is to identify and challenge any negative thoughts or beliefs that may be holding you back. This could involve reframing negative self-talk, working on self-compassion and self-love, or using visualization techniques to envision a positive outcome.

Another helpful strategy is to stay focused on your goals and take consistent action towards achieving them. This may involve setting daily or weekly targets, creating a detailed plan of action, or seeking support from friends or a coach.

Ways to Stay Motivated and Consistent with Your Practice

One of the keys to success with manifestation is to stay motivated and consistent with your practice over time. This may involve finding ways to stay inspired and motivated, such as listening to positive affirmations, reading inspiring books or quotes, or joining a manifestation community.

Another important factor is self-care and taking care of your physical and emotional well-being. This could involve getting enough rest and exercise, eating a healthy diet, practicing mindfulness, or seeking professional support if needed.

In this section, we'll provide practical tips and strategies for troubleshooting your manifestation practice and overcoming common challenges and obstacles. With the right tools and support, you can stay motivated and consistent with your practice and manifest the life of your dreams.

Guided Questions

What are some common challenges or obstacles you've faced while practicing manifestation?

How have you previously dealt with resistance or doubt in your manifestation practice?

What strategies have worked for you in overcoming obstacles or challenges in your manifestation practice?

_____

_____

_____

_____

_____

_____

_____

_____

_____

_____

How can you stay motivated and consistent with your manifestation practice, even when you face setbacks or obstacles?

_____

_____

_____

_____

_____

_____

_____

_____

_____

_____

Are there any limiting beliefs or negative thought patterns that are holding you back from manifesting your desires? How can you challenge and reframe them?

CONCLUSION

As you come to the end of this book, take a moment to reflect on your progress and growth. Celebrate your successes, no matter how small, and recognize the hard work and dedication you have put into your manifestation practice.

Remember that manifestation is an ongoing journey, and there will be ups and downs along the way. Encourage yourself to stay committed to the 369 method and other manifestation practices, even when faced with challenges and obstacles.

In addition to the tools and techniques outlined in this book, there are many resources available for further learning and support. Seek out like-minded individuals, join online communities, and explore additional books and resources to deepen your understanding and practice of manifestation.

You have the power to manifest your desires and create the life you truly want. Keep believing in yourself, stay focused on your goals, and trust in the process. The universe is on your side, and with the right mindset and practices, anything is possible.

BONUS RESOURCES

Thanks for getting this book; here are some bonus resources that help you attract more wealth, love, and abundance to your life:

#1 Download your free report to discover 7 ancient secrets to manifest more wealth, love, and abundance into your life

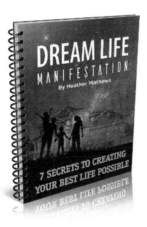

Download your report at
https://manifestabundance.net/dreamlife

#2 Sign up for a free video training to discover how to manifest more wealth, love, and abundance into your life with the "untold method"

Sign up for the free training at

https://manifestabundance.net/freetraining

#3 Download your free mp3 to Removes your "abundance blocks"

Download it at https://manifestabundance.net/mp3

Made in the USA
Las Vegas, NV
03 September 2023

76987456R00142